Common Core Lessor
Health and N

By Carole Marsh

Published by Gallopade International, Inc.

Printed in the U.S.A. (Peachtree City, Georgia)

TABLE OF CONTENTS

G: Includes Graphic Organizer

GO: Graphic Organizer is also available 8½" x 11" online
download at www.gallopade.com/client/go
(numbers above correspond to the graphic organizer numbers online)

Six Classes of Nutrients

Read the text and answer the questions.

The human body needs a number of essential nutrients in order to survive. Essential nutrients are not made by the body. These nutrients have to come from outside sources, usually through your diet. A balanced diet includes the right amount of each essential nutrient your body needs each day. The six essential nutrients are carbohydrates, protein, fat, vitamins, minerals, and water.

Carbohydrates – Carbohydrates provide energy for the body. They are often stored until the body needs them for energy. Carbohydrates are found in breads, whole grains, fruits, and vegetables.

Protein – Protein comes from animal products like meat, fish, milk, and eggs, as well as vegetable sources like beans. Protein is important for repairing and rebuilding the body's tissues.

Fat – Fat provides energy. It also cushions vital organs, helps keep the body warm, and helps the body absorb certain vitamins. The healthiest sources of fat include vegetable-based oils, fish, and nuts.

Vitamins – Vitamins help control important processes in the body. For example, Vitamin K helps blood to clot so cuts stop bleeding quickly. Vitamins are found in all of the food groups. You can also take them in pill form to supplement your diet.

Minerals – Minerals are involved in many body processes such as digestion, bone formation, and heart function. Calcium and iron are examples of essential minerals. Calcium helps build strong bones and teeth. Iron helps make red blood cells, which deliver oxygen all over the body.

Water – Up to 60% of an adult human body is made up of water. Water is essential to the body. It helps transport nutrients to cells. It also helps the body get rid of waste. Besides drinking it, you can get water from foods like soup, or foods with a high water content like fruits and vegetables.

PART A: Use a dictionary to complete the questions below.

1. A. Define <u>essential</u> as it is used in the text.
   B. List a synonym and an antonym for <u>essential</u>.
2. A. Define <u>supplement</u> as it is used in the text.
   B. Explain how vitamins in pill form <u>supplement</u> a person's diet.

PART B: Use the text to determine whether the statements are true or false.

3. Vitamin C is essential for blood clotting.
4. Meat, eggs, and beans are good sources of carbohydrates.
5. Fat is not essential for our diet.
6. Calcium is an essential vitamin for the human body.
7. Protein helps rebuild and repair body tissues.

PART C: Complete the activities.

8. Predict what might happen if someone's body did not receive the six essential nutrients for a long period of time.
9. Create a balanced menu for breakfast, lunch, dinner, and snacks that includes all six essential nutrients. Be specific with your food choices.
10. Some popular diets encourage cutting out carbohydrates. What can you infer about how the body might respond to a reduced amount of daily carbohydrates?
11. Use classroom and online resources to explain the difference between complex and simple carbohydrates.
12. Use classroom and online resources to define Omega-3 fats. What types of food include Omega-3s? Why are Omega-3s important?
13. Imagine you are a nutritionist giving diet advice to a patient. The patient's body has a difficult time absorbing vitamins. What type of essential nutrient would you suggest and why? What specific types of foods should be added to the patient's diet?

Health & Nutrition Vocabulary

Use a dictionary and other resources to complete the graphic organizer for each vocabulary word.

appetite	immunization
calcium	nutrient
calorie	mineral
carbohydrate	obesity
diet	protein
digestion	vitamin

DEFINITION	FACTS/CHARACTERISTICS

WORD

USE THE WORD IN A SENTENCE

Nutrition Label

Most food packages sold in stores have nutrition labels on them. These labels provide easy-to-read nutritional facts for <u>consumers</u>. Analyze the label and answer the questions.

Sample label for Macaroni & Cheese

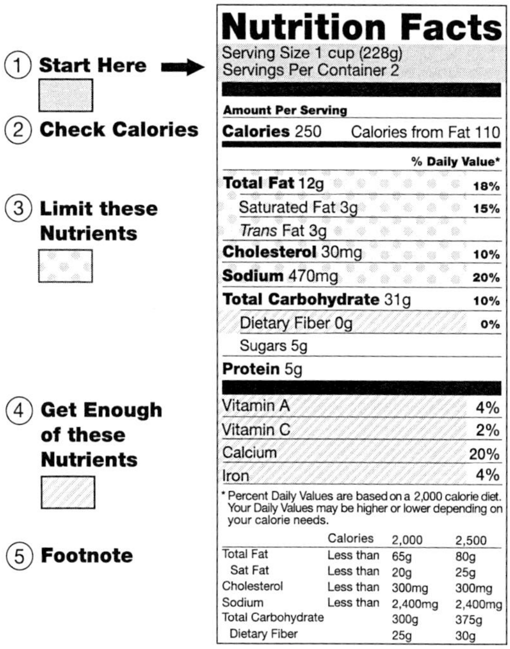

1. A. Define <u>consumers</u> as it is used in the directions.
   B. Why are consumers interested in reading nutrition labels?
2. Almost all food sold in grocery stores includes a Nutrition Facts label similar to this one. List at least 3 ways this information is helpful to know.
3. What happens if you eat more calories than your body uses in a day? Name two ways to solve this problem.
4. Cut out two nutrition labels from some favorite foods you have at home. Attach them to a piece of paper. Compare serving sizes, calories, vitamins, etc. Which food is the best choice for you to eat? Why?

Compare Nutrition Labels

Compare and contrast the two nutrition labels and answer the questions.

Chocolate Chip Cookie

Nutrition Facts	
Serving Size 1 Cookie (5.7g)	
Servings Per Container 12	
Amount Per Serving	
Calories 240	Calories from Fat 110
	% Daily Value*
Total Fat 12g	**19%**
Saturated Fat 8g	**38%**
Trans Fat 0g	
Cholesterol 40mg	**13%**
Sodium 150mg	**6%**
Total Carbohydrate 33g	**11%**
Dietary Fiber 1g	**5%**
Sugars 21g	
Protein 3g	
Vitamin A	4%
Vitamin C	0%
Calcium	4%
Iron	4%

* Percent Daily Values are based on a 2,000 calorie diet. Your Daily Values may be higher or lower depending on your calorie needs.

Mandarin Oranges Fruit Cup

Nutrition Facts	
Serving Size 1 Cup (113g)	
Servings Per Container 2	
Amount Per Serving	
Calories 70	Calories from Fat 0
	% Daily Value*
Total Fat 0g	**0%**
Saturated Fat 0g	**0%**
Trans Fat 0g	
Cholesterol 0mg	**0%**
Sodium 10mg	**0%**
Total Carbohydrate 18g	**6%**
Dietary Fiber <1g	**2%**
Sugars 17g	
Protein 0g	
Vitamin A	0%
Vitamin C	100%
Calcium	0%
Iron	4%

* Percent Daily Values are based on a 2,000 calorie diet. Your Daily Values may be higher or lower depending on your calorie needs.

1. Which product offers a larger serving size? How do you know?
2. Which product provides less fat? Where do you find that information?
3. If someone needs to limit their intake of cholesterol, which product is the best choice? Why?
4. If someone eats two or three times the recommended serving, what should they do when calculating the calories they have consumed?
5. Which product is the healthiest choice? Explain.
6. Imagine you are a newspaper reporter. Write a short article explaining the value of paying attention to nutrition labels when shopping for food.

Benefits of Exercise

Read the text and answer the questions.

Exercise is important to keep your body healthy. Regular exercise helps creates strong muscles and bones and a healthy heart. Exercise can also help you have a happy outlook on life. Exercise can be fun! Many different activities are forms of exercise, such as running, swimming, sports, biking, and yoga.

Fitness has three main elements: endurance, strength, and flexibility. **Endurance** is your body's ability to sustain higher levels of energy, like running, for long periods of time. Aerobic exercise requires oxygen and helps increase endurance. Aerobic exercise makes your heart beat faster and quickens your breathing. Aerobic activity burns fat and strengthens the heart.

Strength is gained through activities that work the muscles, like sit-ups, pushups, bike riding, and even swinging on the monkey bars! Exercises that work the muscles in your arms, legs, back, and abdomen help create stronger muscles. Stronger muscles mean you can do more activity without getting tired.

Flexibility is the ability to move and bend muscles and joints in the body. Stretching is a great way to increase flexibility. Flexible muscles allow a body to be more agile in different types of activities and guard against injuries.

1. A. Define sustain and agile as they are used in the text.
   B. List a synonym and an antonym for each word.
2. Summarize the main idea of the text.
3. List 5 types of sports that kids participate in. Describe how each sport is an aerobic activity.
4. Use online and classroom resources to learn what happens in the brain when you exercise. Then, explain how exercise can boost your spirits.
5. Create a 7-day exercise plan. Describe what type of exercise you will do each day and why you chose it. Make sure you include exercises from each element of fitness. Discuss your plan with the class.

Benefits of Immunization

Read the text, look at the graph and photograph, and answer the questions.

Every child and adult has an immune system to protect against sickness and disease. Some diseases are more dangerous than others. Some serious diseases spread very quickly and are difficult for many people's immune systems to handle. Over the years, scientists created substances called vaccines to help make people immune to certain diseases. People receive vaccines in a shot. This process is known as vaccination, or immunization.

Immunizations give the body immunity, or the power to fight off certain diseases. Immunizations work by introducing small amounts of weak or dead germs that cause a particular disease. For example, the measles vaccine contains a small amount of a weakened measles virus. The vaccine is injected into the body. The body is strong enough to fight off the small amount of measles and remembers it. If the body encounters the measles virus again, the immune system recognizes it and fights it off.

The polio vaccine is an example of how effective immunization can be. Polio is a contagious disease that can cause paralysis, or the inability to move. Polio was very common in the U.S. until the mid 1950s. President Franklin Roosevelt was a victim of polio and could not walk. He had to use a wheelchair, but did not let that stop him from becoming President of the United States!

In 1955, the polio vaccine was introduced. The cases of polio dropped dramatically. Today, polio has been eliminated from most countries in the world.

Courtesy of National Archives and Records Administration

Polio Cases in U.S.
1937-2011

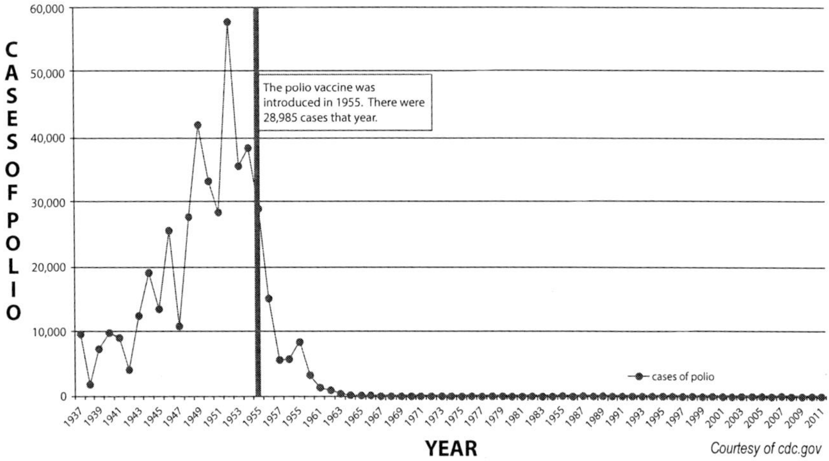

1. Define <u>immune system</u> and <u>contagious</u> as they are used in the text.
2. Summarize the main idea of the text.
3. A. What information does the graph provide?
   B. How does the graph prove the effectiveness of immunizations?
4. What year experienced the highest rate of polio cases?
5. How many fewer polio cases were there in 1968 compared to 1952?
6. What can you infer from the photograph of Franklin Roosevelt about the effects of polio?
7. List some character traits Franklin Roosevelt must have possessed to serve as President of the United States while having polio.
8. A. Based on the text, graph, and picture, do you think the polio vaccine is effective?
   B. Using your answer from part A, what can you infer about the effectiveness of vaccines as a whole?

PRIMARY SOURCE ANALYSIS

Quotes About Health

Analyze the quotes about health and fitness and answer the questions.

"Early to bed, early to rise, makes a man healthy, wealthy, and wise." – Benjamin Franklin

"Let food be thy medicine and medicine be thy food." – Hippocrates

"A good laugh and a long sleep are the best cures in the doctor's book." – Irish Proverb

1. Explain what each quote means to you. Which one do you agree with the most? Why did you choose that quote?
2. A. What important daily activity is Benjamin Franklin promoting in his quote?
   B. How do you feel when you don't get enough sleep? How can that affect your daily life? How do you feel when you sleep well? How can that affect your daily life?
3. From what you have learned about nutrition, explain how food can act as medicine.
4. Describe how a "good laugh" makes you feel. Describe how a sad movie makes you feel. Infer why a "good laugh" is said to be one of the "best cures in the doctor's book."
5. What do Ben Franklin's quote and the Irish Proverb have in common?
6. Create a list of health habits you perform each day. Next to each habit, describe how it benefits your overall health. Do any of your health habits need to change? Proofread and edit your work.

Malnutrition in Our World

Study the map and answer the questions.

Courtesy of doctorswithoutborders.org/2008

1. Use a dictionary to define <u>malnutrition</u>.
2. What information does the map provide?
3. What continents experience the highest rates of malnutrition?
4. Use the map and classroom and online resources to identify the name of each country with more than 15% acute malnutrition.
5. As a class, research and discuss reasons for malnutrition in developing countries. List causes of malnutrition and potential effects of malnutrition. Suggest solutions to the problem.
6. Write a journal entry about how you feel after learning about malnutrition around the world. What emotions do you feel? What actions would you like to take?

Five Food Groups

Complete the graphic organizer by listing five examples of each food group.

Protein

Fruits

Vegetables

Grains

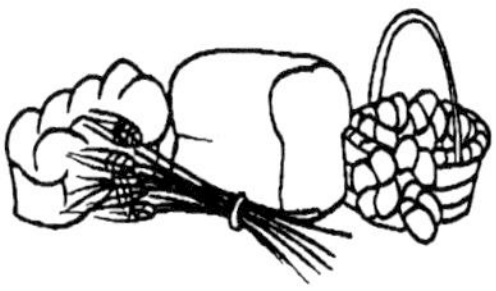

Dairy

Food Pyramid and MyPlate

The food pyramid was originally created by the U.S. Department of Agriculture to show Americans how to eat a balanced diet. The pyramid listed grains as the largest serving group with 6-11 servings a day. Over time, the food pyramid received criticism from nutritionists and scientists. In 2011, the USDA introduced MyPlate, a new way to describe a healthy diet. MyPlate shows suggested serving sizes for each of the five food groups on a sample plate.

Compare and contrast the Food Pyramid with the new MyPlate concept.

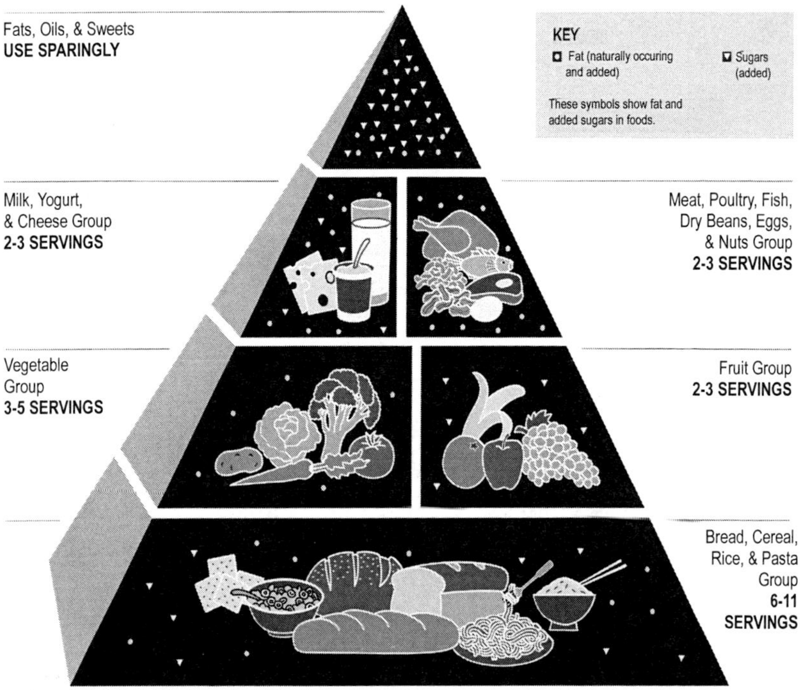

Food Pyramid

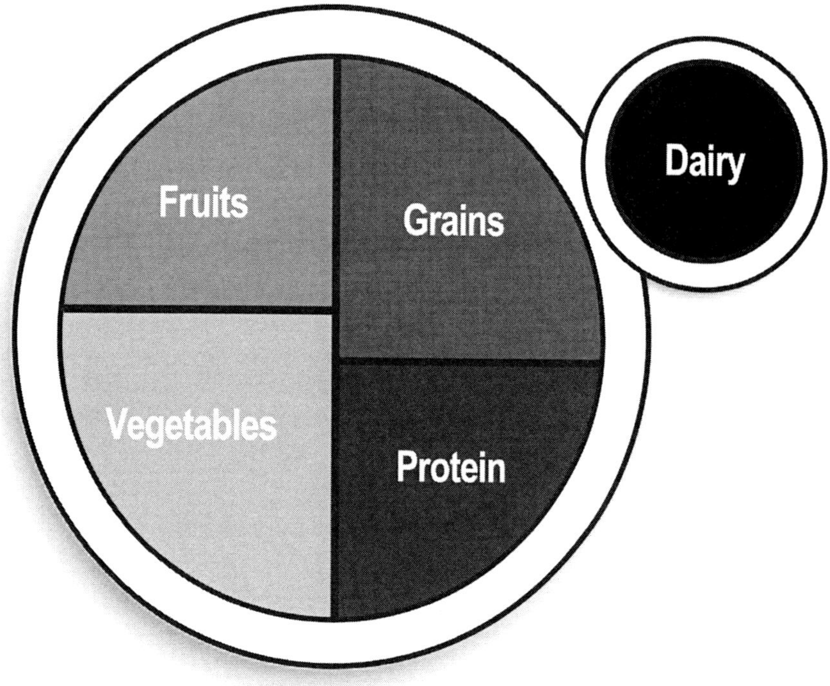

My Plate

1. Identify and list the main differences between the food pyramid and MyPlate. What are the similarities?
2. What can you infer about why some scientists and nutritionists criticized the food pyramid? Cite evidence from the food pyramid and MyPlate to support your answer.
3. Create a daily menu (breakfast, lunch, dinner, snacks) that follows the guidelines of the food pyramid. Be specific with your food choices. Make sure you include the right amount of servings for each food group.
4. Create a plate of food (breakfast, lunch, or dinner) that follows the guidelines of MyPlate. Be specific with your food choices and serving sizes.
5. Write down the food you ate yesterday. Did your diet follow the guidelines of the food pyramid? What about MyPlate? If not, what changes can be made to make your diet compatible with the USDA's food guidelines?

Influences on Food Choices

Read the text and answer the questions.

Many things can influence the healthy choices a person makes. Family, culture, technology, and advertisements all have an impact on how people view diet and exercise.

The first influence on a person's health habits is the family. Each family has a different lifestyle. Some may eat healthy dinners at home every night. Others may eat fast food on the run. Some are involved in sports and activities while others spend time relaxing at home together. Whether healthy or unhealthy, some of the first health habits come from family.

Culture can also affect a person's health behavior. Cultures around the world have very different diets. Asian countries eat large amounts of rice, while countries along the Mediterranean Ocean eat lots of fish, vegetables, and olive oil. American culture is fast-paced. As a result, many Americans eat lots of processed and fast foods in their diet.

Technology affects health habits every day. Many people work on computers. They sit at desks for hours instead of moving. Television and video games also encourage a sedentary lifestyle. However, some technologies, like heart rate and step monitors encourage an active, healthy lifestyle.

Advertising has an enormous effect on food and behavior choices. Commercials, magazines, billboards, and online ads can encourage a wide range of health habits. A picture of a steaming cheese pizza may lead to unhealthy eating while a commercial for a gym can encourage daily exercise.

1. Use a dictionary to define sedentary as it is used in the text. List several synonyms.
2. Search newspapers, magazines, and the Internet for examples of positive and negative health messages from the media. Write a short summary of why each example is positive or negative. Present your examples to the class.
3. Separate into groups. Use a computer to create an advertisement or commercial that encourages healthy eating or a healthy activity. Present it to the class and discuss.

PRIMARY SOURCE ANALYSIS

Food Manufacturers Make a Difference

This text is part of a speech given in 2010 by First Lady Michelle Obama. Mrs. Obama was speaking at the Grocery Manufacturers Association conference. She urged food manufacturers to provide healthier food products, especially those aimed at children.

Read the speech excerpt and answer the questions.

"This is a shared responsibility. That's why I've gone to parents and I've asked them to do their part. They have a responsibility to watch what their kids eat and teach good habits...And all of you have a responsibility as well.

"And we need you not just to tweak around the edges, but to entirely rethink the products that you're offering, the information that you provide about these products, and how you market those products to our children. That starts with revamping or ramping up your efforts to reformulate your products, particularly those aimed at kids, so that they have less fat, salt, and sugar, and more of the nutrients that our kids need.

"As a mom, I know it is my responsibility—and no one else's—to raise my kids. But what does it mean when so many parents are finding that their best efforts are undermined by an avalanche of advertisements aimed at their kids? And what are these ads teaching kids about food and nutrition? That it's good to have salty, sugary food and snacks every day—breakfast, lunch, and dinner?"

1. Summarize the main idea of the speech excerpt.
2. Explain what Mrs. Obama means by "shared responsibility."
3. List 3-5 products you see in the grocery store that are marketed to children.
   A. What details of the packaging show the food is intended for kids?
   B. Are the products you found healthy for kids or not so healthy? (Tip: Read the nutrition labels to be sure.)
4. In your opinion, do most food advertisements you see on television encourage healthy eating in children? Why or why not?

Personal Health and Safety

Read the text and answer the questions.

Good habits that are formed as a child can last a lifetime. Habits that promote health and safety are simple, and they can help you live a happier, longer life. Practicing these habits each day is important. Some examples of healthy habits are:

Wear your seatbelt every time you ride in the car.

Wash your hands before eating, when you handle food, after you cough or sneeze, and after you use the bathroom.

Wear a helmet when riding a bike.

Brush and floss your teeth at least twice a day.

Wear sunscreen when you are out in the sun. Reapply it after swimming or perspiring a lot.

Eat fresh fruits and vegetables every day.

Exercise every day.

Hold the railing when walking up and down stairs.

Get regular check-ups at your doctor.

Drink plenty of water every day.

Limit time in front of the television and computer.

1. A. Use a dictionary to define habit as it is used in the text.
   B. Explain how an action can become a habit.
2. Which habits listed above are safety habits? Which habits are healthy habits? Make a list of each type of habit.
3. List 3 additional health and safety habits that are not listed above.
4. Write a journal entry. First, describe the health and safety habits you use in a typical day. Next, describe some unhealthy habits you'd like to change. Proofread and edit your work.
5. Choose a safety habit from the list. Write a narrative about someone your age who did not follow that safety habit and received a minor injury. Describe the lesson that person learned from their mistake.

Counting Calories

1. Study the chart. 2. Fill in the calorie counts for each food in the three breakfast choices. 3. Answer the questions.

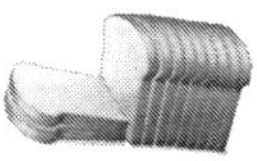

Food	Quantity	Amount of Calories
Omelet with cheese	2 eggs	320
Pancakes with syrup	2 medium	350
Bacon	2 slices	92
Whole wheat toast	1 slice	75
Oatmeal	½ cup	83
Strawberries	½ cup	30
1% Milk	1 cup	105
Orange juice	1 cup	111
Banana	1 medium	105
Eggs (scrambled)	2 large	204

Breakfast 1:
2 eggs ______
Bacon ______
Toast ______
Orange Juice ______
TOTAL Calories ______

Breakfast 2:
Oatmeal ______
Strawberries ______
Eggs ______
1% Milk ______
TOTAL Calories ______

Breakfast 3:
Banana ______
Pancakes ______
Omelet ______
1% Milk ______
TOTAL Calories ______

1. Which breakfast has the least total calories?
2. Which breakfast is the least healthy? Why?
3. Compare 1% milk to whole milk. What is the difference?
4. Create a breakfast from the items listed in the calorie chart that has 414 calories. Include two food choices and one drink choice.
5. Which breakfast provides the most potential energy?
6. Use classroom and online resources to create a calorie chart for your lunch. Look up the calories of each item in your lunch. Add together the total calories. Is your lunch high or low in calories?

Public Health Poster

This poster was created by the city government of Chicago, Illinois, during an influenza epidemic in 1918. Analyze the poster and answer the questions.

Section 1

INFLUENZA
FREQUENTLY COMPLICATED WITH
PNEUMONIA
IS PREVALENT AT THIS TIME THROUGHOUT AMERICA.

Section 2

THIS THEATRE IS CO-OPERATING WITH THE DEPARTMENT OF HEALTH.
YOU MUST DO THE SAME

Section 3

IF YOU HAVE A COLD AND ARE COUGHING AND SNEEZING- DO NOT ENTER THIS THEATRE
GO HOME AND GO TO BED UNTIL YOU ARE WELL
Coughing, Sneezing or Spitting Will Not Be Permitted In The Theatre. In case you must cough or Sneeze, do so in your own handkerchief, and if the Coughing or Sneezing Persists Leave The Theatre At Once.

Section 4

This Theatre has agreed to co-operate with the Department Of Health in disseminating the truth about Influenza, and thus serve a great educational purpose.

Section 5

HELP US TO KEEP CHICAGO THE HEALTHIEST CITY IN THE WORLD
JOHN DILL ROBERTSON
COMMISSIONER OF HEALTH

1. Use a dictionary to define epidemic.
2. Who is the intended audience of the poster? Summarize the message.
3. Where do you think this poster was hung? Include type of business, city, and state. Cite evidence from the text to support your answer.
4. Which sections are informational? Which sections are instructive?
5. Read section 4. Do you think this poster serves a “great educational purpose”? Why or why not?
6. What can you infer about the effectiveness of this poster in preventing the spread of influenza? What other means of communication could businesses have used in 1918 to prevent the spread of disease?

GRAPHIC ORGANIZER

Problem-Solution-Results

Use online and classroom resources to research a health-related problem in America. Ideas include heart disease, lung cancer, or obesity. Use the information you gather to complete the graphic organizer.

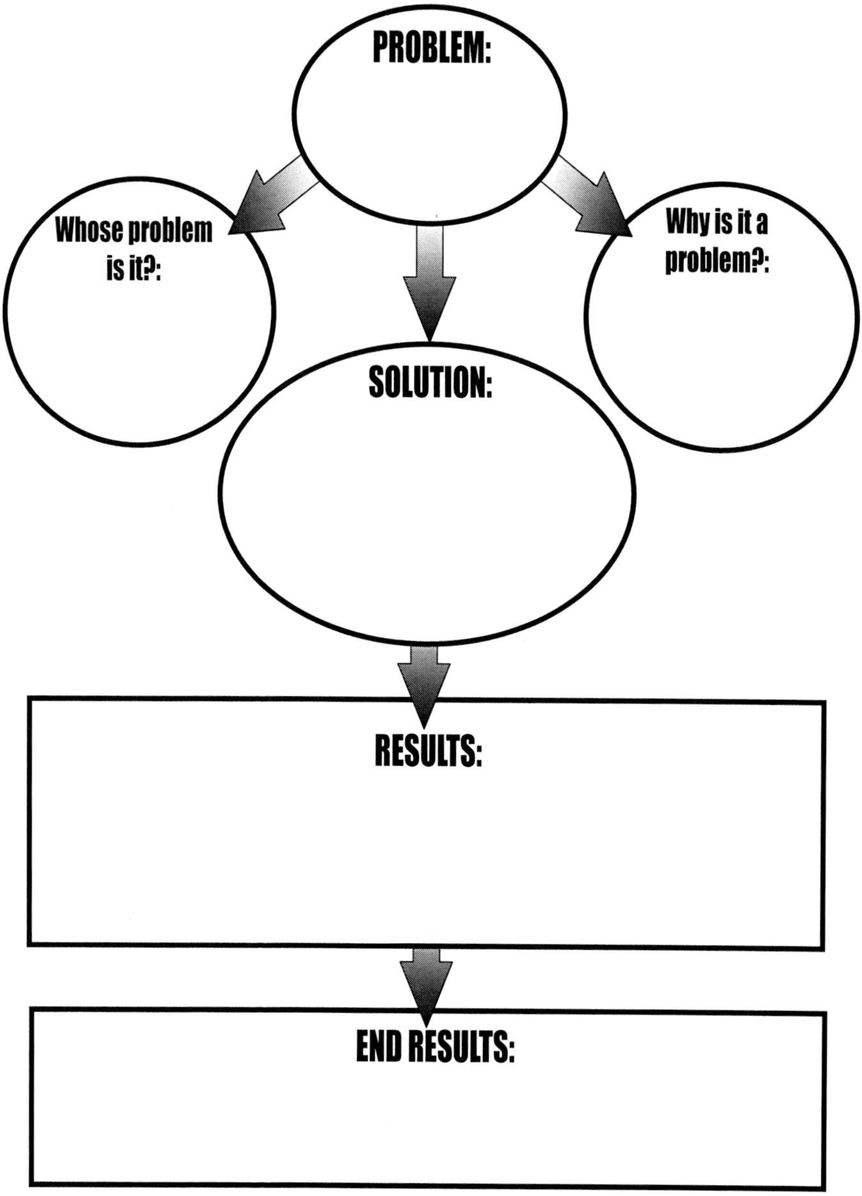

Physical Activity and Heart Disease

Heart disease is the leading cause of death in men and women in America. It is never too early to start taking care of your heart. Your heart is a muscle that works very hard to spread blood through the body. Diet and exercise have a huge impact on heart health. Studies have proven that physically active people have lower rates of heart disease.

Study the maps and answer the questions.

Percent of adults reporting no leisure-time exercise (2013)

Map 1

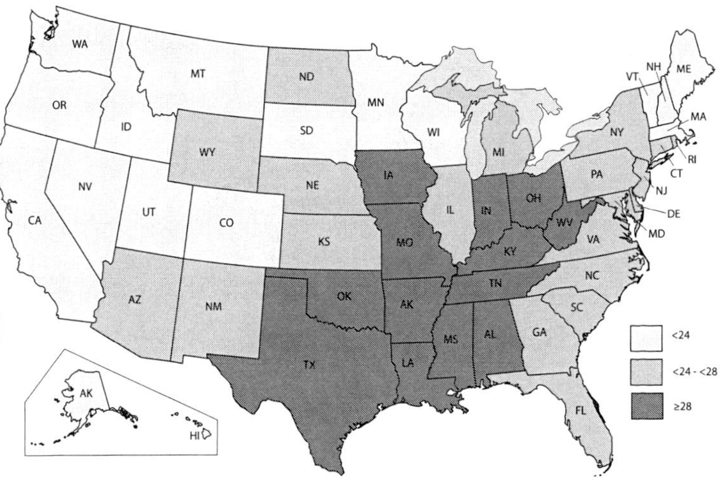

Heart Disease Rates per 100,000, 35+, all races and genders (2008-2010)

Map 2

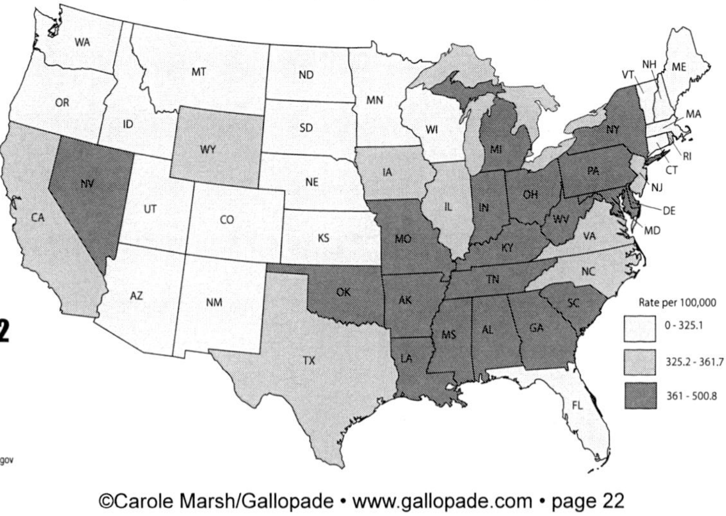

Courtesy of cdc.gov

PART A: Study the maps to determine whether the statements are true or false.

1. Map 1 shows that the states of California, Oregon, and Washington have a large percentage of people who exercise in their leisure time.
2. The dark gray states on Map 2 have the lowest rate of heart disease.
3. Map 2 shows that the highest amount of people who exercise in their leisure time live in the South.
4. Alabama, Mississippi, and Louisiana have high rates of heart disease.
5. Alabama, Mississippi, and Louisiana have low rates of people who exercise in their leisure time.

PART B: Use the text and maps to answer the questions.

6. A. Name 6 states that are dark gray on both maps. In what part(s) of the country are they located?
   B. Name 6 states that are white on both maps. In what part(s) of the country are they located?
7. What parts of the country have the highest rates of heart disease and lowest exercise rates? Circle the correct answer.

   Midwest and South Midwest and West South and West
8. Knowing that physically active people have lower rates of heart disease, what important conclusion can you draw from the data on these maps?
9. What state has a high heart disease rate and a high rate of leisure-time exercise? Is that an unusual trend, according to the maps?

PART C: Complete the activities.

10. A. Separate into groups. Choose a state. Use online resources to research heart health trends and exercise statistics within that state.
    B. Is the state you chose heart-healthy? Why or why not?
11. What are two basic steps people can take to improve their heart health? Discuss as a class.
12. Choose a state with unhealthy heart disease rates. Write an editorial (opinion article) for a newspaper in that state urging citizens to make changes to improve their heart health.

Correlations to Common Core State Standards

For your convenience, correlations are listed page-by-page and for the entire book!

This book is correlated to the Common Core State Standards for English Language Arts grades 3-8, and to Common Core State Standards for Literacy in History, Science, & Technological Subjects grades 6-8.

Correlations are highlighted in gray.

PAGE #	READING *Includes:* RI: Reading Informational Text RH: Reading History	WRITING *Includes:* W: Writing WHST: Writing History, Science, & Technology	LANGUAGE *Includes:* L: Language LF: Language Foundational Skills	SPEAKING & LISTENING *Includes:* SL: Speaking & Listening
2-3	RI RH . **1** 2 **3** **4** 5 6 7 8 9 **10**	W WHST . 1 **2** **3** **4** 5 6 **7** 8 **9** **10**	L LF . 1 2 3 **4** **5** **6**	SL . 1 2 3 4 5 6
4	RI RH . 1 2 3 **4** 5 6 7 8 9 **10**	W WHST . 1 2 3 **4** 5 6 7 8 9 10	L LF . 1 2 3 **4** 5 **6**	SL . 1 2 3 4 5 6
5	RI RH . **1** 2 3 **4** **5** 6 **7** 8 9 10	W WHST . 1 **2** 3 **4** 5 6 7 **8** 9 **10**	L LF . 1 2 3 **4** 5 **6**	SL . 1 2 3 4 5 6
6	RI RH . **1** 2 **3** 4 **5** 6 **7** 8 **9** **10**	W WHST . 1 **2** **3** **4** 5 6 7 **8** **9** **10**	L LF . 1 2 3 4 5 6	SL . 1 2 3 4 5 6
7	RI RH . **1** **2** **3** **4** 5 6 7 8 9 **10**	W WHST . **1** **2** 3 **4** 5 6 **7** **8** **9** **10**	L LF . 1 2 3 **4** 5 **6**	SL . **1** 2 3 **4** 5 **6**
8-9	RI RH . **1** **2** **3** **4** 5 **6** **7** **8** **9** **10**	W WHST . 1 **2** 3 **4** 5 6 7 8 **9** **10**	L LF . 1 2 3 **4** 5 **6**	SL . 1 2 3 4 5 6
10	RI RH . **1** **2** 3 4 5 6 7 **8** **9** **10**	W WHST . **1** **2** 3 **4** **5** 6 7 **8** **9** **10**	L LF . 1 2 3 4 **5** **6**	SL . 1 2 3 4 5 6
11	RI RH . **1** 2 3 4 5 6 **7** 8 9 **10**	W WHST . **1** 2 3 **4** 5 6 **7** **8** **9** **10**	L LF . 1 2 3 **4** 5 **6**	SL . **1** **2** 3 **4** 5 **6**
12-13	RI RH . 1 2 3 **4** 5 6 **7** 8 9 **10**	W WHST . 1 2 3 4 5 6 7 **8** 9 10	L LF . 1 2 3 4 5 6	SL . 1 2 3 4 5 6
14-15	RI RH . 1 2 3 4 **5** 6 **7** 8 **9** **10**	W WHST . 1 **2** 3 **4** 5 6 7 **8** **9** **10**	L LF . 1 2 3 4 5 **6**	SL . 1 2 3 4 5 6
16	RI RH . 1 2 3 4 5 6 **7** **8** **9** **10**	W WHST . **1** **2** **3** **4** 5 **6** **7** **8** **9** **10**	L LF . 1 2 3 **4** 5 **6**	SL . **1** **2** 3 **4** **5** **6**
17	RI RH . **1** **2** 3 4 5 **6** 7 8 9 **10**	W WHST . **1** **2** 3 **4** 5 6 7 **8** 9 **10**	L LF . 1 2 3 **4** 5 **6**	SL . 1 2 3 4 5 6
18	RI RH . **1** 2 3 **4** **5** 6 **7** **8** 9 **10**	W WHST . 1 **2** **3** **4** **5** 6 7 **8** **9** **10**	L LF . 1 2 3 **4** 5 **6**	SL . 1 2 3 4 5 6
19	RI RH . **1** 2 3 4 5 6 **7** 8 **9** **10**	W WHST . 1 **2** 3 **4** 5 6 **7** **8** **9** **10**	L LF . 1 2 3 4 5 6	SL . 1 2 3 4 5 6
20	RI RH . **1** **2** **3** **4** **5** 6 **7** **8** 9 **10**	W WHST . 1 **2** 3 **4** 5 6 7 8 **9** **10**	L LF . 1 2 3 **4** 5 **6**	SL . 1 2 3 4 5 6
21	RI RH . 1 2 **3** 4 **5** 6 7 8 9 **10**	W WHST . 1 2 3 4 5 6 **7** 8 **9** **10**	L LF . 1 2 3 4 5 6	SL . 1 2 3 4 5 6
22-23	RI RH . **1** 2 **3** 4 5 6 **7** 8 9 **10**	W WHST . 1 **2** 3 **4** 5 6 **7** 8 **9** **10**	L LF . 1 2 3 4 5 **6**	SL . **1** 2 3 **4** 5 **6**
COMPLETE BOOK	RI RH . **1** **2** **3** **4** **5** **6** **7** **8** **9** **10**	W WHST . **1** **2** **3** **4** **5** **6** **7** **8** **9** **10**	L LF . 1 2 3 **4** **5** **6**	SL . **1** **2** 3 **4** **5** **6**

For the complete Common Core standard identifier, combine your grade + "." + letter code above + "." + number code above.

In addition to the correlations indicated here, the activities may be adapted or expanded to align to additional standards and to meet the diverse needs of your unique students!